A Letter to Serafin

AKRON SERIES IN POETRY

a wszystko wymagało ciągn
coby tam postać sam sobą roz m
pomisli i doradzi jak zostawić
siłach ale i na oczy mgło za ciąg
a tym czasem pokornie dziękuj
jeszcze przy dobrej pamięnci Żeg
was wszystkich dla pana jezu
ktury cierpiał otkupienie
dla nas wszystkich a trzyman
jak umrzem nie przyente modl
na kościoły nie dawał żeby w
teraz rozmyslam w dzien i w noc
żym a szczym Bog dobrotliwy w
żadnych kolegow niema o któr
Źrozie Brastaskie po umiera
siostra kozłoska rok temu jak
i nie widziała taki nasz rodz
was wszystkich Panu Bo

A Letter to Serafin

John Minczeski

The University of Akron Press
Akron, Ohio

 • First Edition 2009 • Manufactured in the United States of America. • All inquiries and permission requests should be addressed to the Publisher, the University of Akron Press, Akron, Ohio 44325-1703.

13 12 11 10 09 5 4 3 2 1

LIBRARY OF CONGRESS CATALOGING-IN-PUBLICATION DATA
Minczeski, John.

A letter to Serafin / John Minczeski.

P. CM. — (Akron series in poetry)

ISBN 978-1-931968-68-3 (pbk. : alk. paper)

I. Title.

PS3563.I4635L48 2009

811'.54—DC22

2009014029

The paper used in this publication meets the minimum requirements of American National Standard for Information Sciences—Permanence of Paper for Printed Library Materials, ANSI Z39.48–1984. ∞

Cover: *Dynamic clouds,* Tadeusz Gadza. Used by permission of the artist.

Contents

November

A Letter to Serafin

for Joan

A Letter from Serafin

ronisława aiuważam z nicht
n jak się obrocic niech Bronisła
szystkich bo co raz gorzej nie to co n
ispamienici codzien inaczej
Bogu i to bie za pamiencia pier
ię z wami i cs cało rodzino połę
tri Boskiej i swientego Józefa
ego swiata to jest nay ważniejsze
na pokontzyemy pożniej nie po
sby i aoby łsię za cwe skąpstwo
to jak uważam dużo mamy nie poszło
zeba stanąc przed sądem Bo-
m dłużej to twientkszepytanie.
roz miawiał na łoncew kabyc
e i panioze f jednego roky rodz
eta ale sz nie znała nikogo
czerstwości nie ma po lecar
ało rodzino Zostaje życzliwy
Serafin minczewski

Farm, 1962

Each October, they plumb the black soil
for beets and turnips and carrots.
It is not a harvest so much as a heap

in a horse-drawn cart. They ride
to town with potatoes to trade for clothes,
potatoes for Sunday offering.

They wouldn't mind riding to America
like my grandfather who's returned
with a suitcase crammed with cigarettes and toilet paper,

who sits in the wagon with his brother
and the potatoes. In the foreground, children
wear my coat from two winters before,

my brother's snowsuit, dresses from my cousins.
The linings where my grandfather stashed tens
and twenties have been ripped open

and resewn. Maybe they'll pay off
the overseer to overlook their poaching in the forest,
buy another horse to share with neighbors.

My grandfather's Polish, fifty years out of date,
still works like an old Ford. They look
at the camera, my father snaps the shutter.

With their cigarettes and their smiles,
Hello, America. In three years, my grandfather
will begin coughing up blood.

Outside the church in Sokółka, the names
on the family stone will stop with his brother, age ninety-two.
There is no room for new names.

Annunciation

What is she reading at her stand-up desk—
the Psalms maybe, the Song of Songs—

the morning an angel, feathers trembling
like aspen leaves, appears?

The fragrance of his lily so overwhelms her,
she can barely hear.

Golden rays penetrate
with none of the usual trickery—

no ride on the bull, no rain of gold—
just two fingers he points at her,

light that makes her wince, a quick
Ave Maria, and the world

has changed. No enormous bird,
just a shimmer that became

a beautiful man, her book's pages
fluttering in that sudden wind.

She holds a hand up to ward it off,
then both hands on her belly,

the name of the father
never to be spoken.

October Primrose

Its green flag now red,
it holds its own against turning maples
like an old partisan song.
Remember the black butterfly

of summer, stuck in the craw
of heat? Today
no one holds these leaves
against the sky.

They have abandoned
green camouflage for this
one chance to pledge
allegiance to the ground, to bugs

tending them during blossom season.
And now, under the bloomed-out
phlox, the brittle khaki stalks
of daylilies, like the remains

of downed Cessnas, the red
of bull-vaulters in the museum
at Irakleon, not the ambitious rust
of asters but the glowing sword

of the Archangel after the fire's gone out,
some Eden begins slipping back
into the world like a cluster of leaves going nova—
a gash, an open wound in the air.

Let other leaves turn yellow
and scabby brown; let morning
glories go full-throttle until frost,
and yellow jackets without exit strategies

continue trading in the spot market
of the trash can. The primrose,
red shift in the spectrum,
has nowhere to go but here.

Michelangelo: Leda and Zeus

Here's Michelangelo, ladies and gentlemen,
squirreling around the old candy store of myth,
it being the Renaissance and all,
with a female nude for a change;

and here's Zeus, roving the planet like a talent scout
looking for the most beautiful woman
to reward. Hard to say how long he had her
in the crosshairs before making his move,

how many advances she spurned
before he hit on the swan thing. She's actually flattered
he settled beside her with so little fear,
laying his head on her lap.

And the feathers—Zeus outdid himself
on this one—soft as sea foam as she strokes them.
It can't be long before she's flat on her back,
and it's pointless to resist—her mother

never told her about swans.
That is what Michelangelo wanted,
the god not being such a churl
that she can't have her fun, too,

a rapture that moves the god to touch beak
to lips, or between them, exchanging breath.
She clenches her arm around his neck
to keep him from rising to heaven

without her. O, she must know nothing
can stop him, just as nothing can stop her
from keeping him earthbound one moment longer.

Kraków

Walking past the Vis à Vis bar
a whiff from a Gauloise pulled me up short.
I breathed the acrid smell
as though it couldn't harm me

and held it, the way the vain
hold onto lost youth. There were
Braques and Mondrians;
there was Giovanna driving Uro

to the airport, giving him a carton
of *Caporal Bleu* before he left Rome for good.
Back in the present moment
seasoned with street musicians,

She loves you, yeah, yeah, yeah,
the sun still climbed through October.
There were rats, for certain,
but no one saw them. Maybe I became

invisible as I once was, sixth grade,
when I could look at no one
and be safe. Later, in Florence,
a waiter ignored me, an American

whose country was pimping another war.
It only seemed like the end of the world.
I cannot say the name of the street in Kraków
that moment which turned into other moments—

espresso, a brioche in a bar, the first tobacco hit
in the morning when I was twenty and invincible.
I'd just seen Leonardo's *Lady with an Ermine,*
the gallery of contemporary art being closed

for updating. The light fell on us, on me.
The sun kept climbing.
The rats maintained invisibility.
Nothing could be further from the truth.

Relics

We can't help but hoard them—the Mickey Mantle
rookie card, mint copy of the first *X-Men*—
but something from a saint was extra,

a get-out-of-hell-free token, the super rich
snapping them up by the gross to grease the eye
of that needle they'd have to squeeze through

before the golden stairway. They commissioned
shrines and tiny altars for a scrap
of St. Agatha's veil, index finger

John the Baptist pointed to Jesus with.
Relics were the rage, they were everywhere,
they must have worked.

She sat in the back row on the flight to Rome,
speaking of her pilgrimage to Padre Pio's monastery
before starting a new round of chemo. Having lost

both parents, a brother, and daughter
to cancer, her odds, she figured,
hovered at zero. A visit to the Vatican

was out, ditto for Assisi—opportunities
for miracles were, like her time,
in short supply. I saw her again

at *Stazione Termini*, waiting for a train
to the monastery. She sat alone,
clinging to that moment. Her son

wandered the food kiosks,
grazing on a ham and cheese, his last
before home-grown artichokes and sautéed chicory.

If there's a half-life left in that finger,
you who wandered, half-crazed,
wearing the skins of hyenas and jackals

out of the desert, point it
at her. Make like laser, make
like fire. If the batteries

in that leathery finger are still good,
fire it, you who have nothing
left to prove.

Tree Lilac in Blossom

Nearby, a bee's motor stops and starts
like a tattooing needle from petal to petal,
O, not-so-tall-tree-of-the-ear.
I sit under as though wearing it,

not to hide from the sun,
but to feel its brief absence
through the leaves' absorption,
in the miniscule blossoms floating in my coffee.

What is missing today? Not slugs,
those revelers of wet summers,
nor cumulus, always with us.

A peregrine drifts over, roving.
A million unhinged rotors float down,
smearing the world with pollen.

Prophet

woe onto him that saith to the wood, awake;
to the dumb stone, arise
Habakkuk 2:19

Among statues of prophets in the Baptistry—beards gnarled
as oak bark, scrolls they hold like mirrors to the people—
this one is clean-shaven and bald as a pumpkin,
his hands hanging down like acorns. If the lord says *go,*

he goes. Should he flee, the lord will reel him back
like a bad cast. Sometimes the lord waits
invisible as air, as a dull ache. Someone has given him
a heel of bread and a sardine. He hopes the lord

will not call before he's finished eating.
Will the lord mind his fishy breath? When he opens his mouth,
he doesn't know whose voice he'll hear, so he remains
silent. He wrote what he was told, now he looks on the doomed

going about their daily business. Though the lord
has given him to see the invaders, their horses like leopards
about to attack, he is not, all told, a bad man.

Abraham

For once, I'd like to ask why this business
of killing a son is so delectable. I accept
the obedience part, the ritual knife,
stone altar. But why truss the boy

like a fatted calf? Yes, the storm overhead
could be the all-seeing watching me place a rag
over my son's face, to avoid his silent pleading
before I thrust into his neck.

And after, in that killing place,
would lightning flash down like a tongue
to lap the blood?

It might be enough to know
the sacrifice nourished the gods
like smoke rising from battlefields,
but I don't need any more parables.

For once, I'd like to know what would happen
if I declined: no tricks; no adopting a lamb
or goat, killing *it* instead. Something polite
but firm—*I know you're my God and everything,*

but I can't keep doing your killing for you.
Would he make our drought go on indefinitely?
And if he were to say, *Congratulations, you finally passed,*

I'd still like him to show the angel waiting,
in case I'd gone ahead with it, to stop me before
I could nick that beloved neck, to say *there, there now;*
to take the knife from my shaking hand.

A Letter from My Great-Grandfather, Serafin Minczewski

He was dying and never knew *I'd* get it
across the divide of his death and my birth,
in his native dialect, in his Białystok,
the freshly cobbled road, farmhouse
of squared fir, a village named
for a city in the mountains

but flat as the sheet he wrote on
margin to margin like a ploughed field,
as stingy with paper as he was with land,
emptiness being the playground
of the devil.

Too rushed for punctuation,
his thoughts flashed like rain past his window
before splashing in puddles,

rippling as one thought joined the whole
pond of them

> *every day went to the forest*
> *and everything was paid*
>
> *then it was easier to do business in the night*
> *than now it is in the day*

Like rain falling eighty years that now lands in me.
The sky blue and dry, an enormous
wishbone of blue, and his words
slosh inside. The little waterfalls
of his thoughts grow large as bison
grazing in the forests nearby.

You go in the forest
with a stone, you return
with a rabbit; you go with a sack
for mushrooms.

waited for a story
he writes,

in the letter there was nothing

—a photo of my grandfather's new Ford,
not twenty dollar bills—

it has not arrived in Białystok yet
sent again
he had to withdraw 200 marks

the present local counsel is a company
false as Grodno banks
which are bribable and false

—money was a flock of crows
rising up
when they saw him coming

I am thinking all the time
how to behave
Bronisław

he writes my grandfather

please give me advice
on how to leave you all

mist covers my eyes
memory worsening

—ready
to go under the black stone
his family will share
(wife, Antonina; daughter, Leonarda;
son, Jan),

the pen ploughing paper
(dictated to a daughter?)

I do not let on
I do not know

when goes back
or stays

the worry over money
playing like a scratchy violin.

There are no receipts to clutch
like a coin between his teeth
to bribe the lesser angels

it is not like being strong
this is our kind

not very tough

from the soil of Jelenie Góra,
where a grandson tends cabbages and turnips
as the family has for centuries

the silence begins with his name in full,
serafin minczewski
signed on the single wing of the page,
a scarecrow's glove.

u kladu ienka opisania to m
szystko wymagało ciągnąć
y tam postać sam sobo roz mista
nisli i doradzi jak zostawić was
ch ale i na oczy mgło zaciągnąć
m czasem pokornie dziękuje pa
ze przy dobrej pamięci żegnam
s wszystkich dla pana Jezusa

re utrzymały otkupienie ca
nas wszystkich utrzymanie i ob
umrzem nieprzyjente modły i p
kościoły nie dawał żeby w domu
z roz mysłam w dzień i w nocy że
a szczym Bog dobrotliwy wie c
ych kolegow niema s ktorem
zie brastaskie po umierali st
tra kortoska rok temu jak um
e widziała taki nasz rodzaj z
as wszystkich Panu Bogu

One Version

A trickle of water
through a cast-iron radiator,
like the examined life
ruminating on itself,

the only sound of the afternoon
if you don't count the red oaks
clattering, or breath
in the perfect leaf-veins of your lungs,

the world calm
facing the invasions of night. In 1939,
Romuald Minczewski surrendered
with his regiment to the Soviets,

thinking they'd repel the Germans together.
They gave him, in the Katyn woods,
a way out
with a bullet to his head.

My cousin, Józef, told me this
in his dining room where English
was a dusty glass in the cupboard.
No one knew the secret pact

to divide Poland again.
We want to think we'd help,
but the time machine,
if it's been invented,

has fallen into the wrong hands,
and dirt still packs
the holes in those skulls.
The only clouds

are the crowns of those oaks
rattling the last dry leaves,
reeds in the wind, a stream
rippling beneath.

The Camps

> *This is camp law:*
> *People going to their deaths*
> *must be deceived to the very end.*
> *This is the only permissible form of charity.*
> —Tadeusz Borowski, *This Way for the Gas, Ladies and Gentlemen*

1. Auschwitz

Winter lasted forever
for those never heard from again,
their daily ration of coal as meager
as a bowl of thin soup.

But this October, in the suburbs of Kraków,
the air crisp as celery, the sky
sparks over maples that do not turn red;
horse-drawn carts creak on the side of the road

under loads of turnips and rutabagas
as they have for a thousand years.

A kiosk at the entrance displays books
in English and Polish, posters, a rack
of picture postcards. *Get what you need here,*
a fellow tourist visiting a second time says,

you won't find another gift shop
anywhere on this tour. We get
two rolls of Kodachrome, a bottle of water.
Should I *know* what I'm doing here,

standing at the pit of history under *Arbeit Macht Frei*
as Joan frames it in the camera? Other tourists,
fresh from the orientation movie,
flood through. I am unable,

even now in the privileged future,
to go in without her.
Looking down cypress-lined boulevards
away from the barbed wire, the brick barracks

could be campus dorms. It is too easy to imagine
gerbera daisies by the front doors, rows of rust-
colored zinnias and dahlias gracing the road
to Crematorium #1.

Trains pulled in hourly. Smokestacks
pumped around the clock with lubricated precision.
Prisoners, in striped pajamas worn to zero,
took their suitcases. *Hush,*

they said in Polish.
Take this hanger—you must remember its number.
Your clothes will be disinfected and returned
when you finish your shower.

Tooth brushes
clothes brushes
shaving brushes
shoe brushes

Baby shoes
baby bottle nipples
entered in ledgers
with so little time in our lives

pitchers
wash basins
eyeglasses
crutches

prosthetheses
spent cans of Zyclon B
catalogued and examined
and under glass.

Told to label their suitcases,
they wrote in large, block letters

MARIE KAFKA
OTTO ISRAEL SCHÖNHOF
WEISS, GEORG

the tour keeps moving
I cannot copy more.

2. Wooden Barracks, Birkenau

The wind through the open eaves said nothing.
The furnaces with broken tunnels

running down the center of this kennel
spoke no word.

The scab of night wasn't any better
than the open wound of day.

A faint smell filled the barn.
I, who had a return ticket

to pizza and vodka
in the underground cellars of Kraków,

would be rid of it by morning.
If there was a window

I could have thrown it open
and flapped like one of those crows

perched above the statue of Kopernikus
under the light of unknown stars

as though I could be any more successful
in piecing the shattered fragments

of that century—or anything—
together again.

3. Wooden Barracks/2

How could I write about them when the notes
I scribbled in the shorthand of the moment
were like electrons fumbling toward eternity?

How many of my carpenter cousins,
with wooden pegs instead of valuable nails,
joined timbers for the barracks of Birkenau?
And how many, after the Nazis fled, did they dismantle?

The houses they built from that lumber
must still front a street or field. Is there a word
in any language for the perfect conscience

of wood? The few intact barracks turned black
under soot and history. Among the acres of ruins,
chimneys remain standing like weeds
after the unmentionable harvest.

4. Tour Bus

I wanted the bus to leave without us.
I wanted to wander as though I'd lost my mind,
picking stones from the rail bed
under the gate to Camp #2.

I wanted to forfeit the remainder
of my ticket to see if I could get back
with only a Visa and a handful of Złotys.
I wanted to break free

and make my own way
to the present world.
I wanted to lie down and curl
into the earth and have it not be a disaster.

Was it a sudden discomfort
at hearing my own language spoken on the bus?
Or the forensics of silence,
the violent shades of white,

a lingering hangover from the war,
the haze of it still hiding the horizon?
I didn't want to know the way home.
I wanted to follow any scent

rather than continue obeying
the tour guide, no matter how patient
she was. But she held
the bus,

ready to send out searchers,
knowing there are those of us
who have to keep our ears pressed
against brick and wood,

thinking we could spend another hour,
or night,
or the rest of our lives here.

5. November

The day seeps in, Venus riding high at dawn,
both hands on the handlebars, gunning it, hard.

Night lingers in a cup of black coffee,
stars remain etched in frosted windshields.

November: a jukebox of crows,
a dog barking at the wild universe.

In this country where we welcome
the value of distance, the ancient,

wooden smell of Birkenau lingers:
maybe a remnant of coal,

not the rags worn by prisoners.
Does forgiveness have a smell?

Did the circling angel of hope
leave anything besides dust

and the morning trills of jays
in leafless trees?

n iadał tenka opisania ton

szystko wymagało ciągnąno

y tam postać sam sobą roz mistl

nisli i doradzi jak zostawić was

ch ale i na oczy mgło zaciągnąć

m czasem pokornie dziękuję pa

cze przy dobrej pamięci żegnam

s wszystkich dla pana Jezusa

ve utrzymały otkupienie ca

nas wszystkich utrzymanie i ob

umrzem nieprzyjente modły i p

kościoły niedawał żeby wdomu

k rozmyślam w dzień i w nocy że

e oszczym Bóg dobrotliwy wie c

ych kolegów niema z którem

zie Brastaskie po umierali si

tra kortoska rok temu jak um

e widziała taki nasz rodzaj ż

as wszystkich Panu Bogu

Tree Lilac: Dust

The blossoms turn to dust
in cracks between patio bricks—
dust and mud and air.

The blooms keep dropping,
the mosquitoes rising
as I clean my varnish brush.

Steady as she goes. June 22.
Mars is a blazing push pin;
the tree lilac, a magnet. Hummingbirds,
a brush dripping mineral spirits
from the branches, the ground

receiving it all: who are you
to think of resisting just now?

Madonna with the Outline of a Breast

Anonymous, 12th or 13th Century

Somebody had to paint it,
the son of god wrapping
his lips around a nipple as earnestly
as any earthly cousin.

What, anyway, was the point
of getting born without the full
manifesto of family arguments
over dinner, or Giada
taking a first bite

of grilled peach with prosciutto
on the Food Channel.
The monks themselves prepared meals
worthy of the son of man
should he reappear in their midst,

but how portray the infant J.
at the joy of the breast without letting on
how joyful, tempting us further?
The artist must have muttered *breast,*

breast, breast as he drew the bleak outline,
against the modeled flesh of the baby
who shows a wisdom beyond his years,
as if he'd just spoken to those broken

on the wheels of power.
And the mother? The sufferings
of this world have already
worn her eyes opaque.

Leonarda

She fell out of a tree.
Or scarlet fever broke the surge
in her body before she was ten,
stranding her at three and a half feet.
She could handle a goat.
She could throw stones at a wolf.
She was the name that meant bad luck,
like a deaf aunt
who also never married. Lord,
that we may live through years
of no phones or tractors or gasoline.
She painted St. Christopher
crossing the water.
Religion had already gotten him
as it had gotten her.
Religion and gardening.
Religion and canning. She stood on a chair
working alongside women
sweating tomato juice and strawberries.
They filled jars with galaxies of pickles.
Nations of beets.
She painted poppies that grew
in the open cathedral of the sun.
She made her own paints before
the word *organic* had been invented.
Boys her age joined the home army;
they worked in secret factories, aware
they had been sentenced *in absentia*.

She disappeared among
the children when Gestapo swept
up defectives. She taught children
to draw their names
with the Roman alphabet. Holding
the hands of young widows,
she tracked
the decaying orbits of their dead.

Jewish Cemetery, Rymanów

> How many dead people
> are buried in that cemetery,
> *my wife's father asked once*
> *as they drove past.*
>
> *Falling for the gag, she began counting*
> *the stones holding the dead in place.*
> Give up? All of them.

I came among lowering skies
and one-way streets as though looking
for part of myself. My friends
led through tansy,

the medicinal smell rising
as we brushed past to stand
facing inscriptions I couldn't read,
the stones twisting into earth

beneath the storks' empty nests.
As many as on the bus to Kraków?
As many as rags hung on fences
to scare birds on windy days?

Not here, but in the Catholic cemetery
across the road where we parked the car,
families knelt to anoint graves
with carnations and roses.

All evening, lit by votive candles,
the cemetery levitated
as though the souls themselves were rising,
rising and burning.

Judith and Holofernes

Easy enough to sweet-talk her way
into the Assyrian camp and slink into his tent.
Easy for him to guess she was tendered
by a city anxious to appease his fury.

He says, *Look at what the gods*
have sent! After hacking through
enemy lines all day, why *not* relax?
His sentries have owl eyes,

and pikes sharper than owl talons.
The lady and her maid kneel,
feeding him dates dipped in honey,
giving him mouthfuls of wine

from their own lips, first one, then the other—
nibbling his ears. She's not
the pious Judith, beseeching heaven
for help. She's the loosened blouse,

the barefoot dance. She's the *Let me*
show how we prefer
powerful men like you. The one who,
the second time he nods off,

saws through trachea and carotids
as though carving a turkey.
Suddenly sober, he tries to suck breath
as he hears the blood gush from his brain.

Last thing he sees, good observer that he is,
is the inside of a wicker basket the women carry
through camp, past guards and their smirks,
into the comfort of darkness.

Resort Town

Snow tonight, and the bombing of Iraq
resumes each time I turn on the TV,
the snow beginning to stick,
the pavement glaze over.

On the muted screen, the president's trying
not to look smug as enemy cities fall
and troops mass outside Baghdad.
Each summer, this resort rakes in a fortune

from golf courses and walleye lakes. In winter,
they comp a few rooms to artists
who visit the school in town.

Years before, on a crowded bus to Fiesole,
a man began grinding against you—*do something,*
your eyes said. I might have killed him
with a pocket knife if so many passengers

hadn't crammed between us. I stood over
my thirteen-year-old as though guarding her.
Maybe I was. Now, in Nisswa, the snow continues
like a failed defense against the night, and I am alone

after a day of first graders whose permanent teeth
have erupted from pulpy gums.
Even if I'd had my Swiss Army knife out,
blade down and locked, even if I could have reached him,

I wouldn't have slipped it into his heart, regardless
of his fluttering eyelids. It was March and hot.
Everyone watched him get off to gloat at the bus stop
as he buttoned his overcoat.

The stars will have to stand in judgment,
and at this moment they are falling—
a momentary glitter, a triumph of road slush.

The Davids

1. Bernini

Who wouldn't feel a little squirmy,
standing in the line of fire, the marble boy
all tensed and coiled and ready to spring,
lion who's taken two steps before lunging—

a growl, a squint focusing—O, everything—on his target,
as King Saul's vain armor lays at his feet.
Bernini, too young to turn down this commission,
modeled his own scowling face—

at the Cardinal's suggestion? Holding the mirror
like a scalpel to admire the sculptor
who could be picking off rats in Via Montorio,

he'd get chills every time Bernini, still glowering,
looked up to lock eyes—
the rage of an entire people burning behind them.

2. Michelangelo

Calm as a card shark sitting down
to the World Series of Poker,
holding his sling casually over his shoulder

like a beach towel, there's no snarl,
just a good arm and plenty of ammunition
underfoot. He's got prophecy behind him
and generations of Greek statuary.

Hanging at his side, a right hand
blown all out of proportion. Heroes beware,
lest you become heretical.

3. Donatello

The boy, slender body, nipped waist,
has called out
the weapon of mass destruction.

So you send out this girl?
The giant bellows in reply.
Come to papa, Sweetie.

Don't cry, it won't
take long.
And kerpow.

In the oft-repeated phrase
of the Bush administration,
Who'd have guessed

Goliath had a glass forehead?
A knot the size of your fist

forms before he keels over,
a toppled mast in the desert.
They all stand as stunned

as gelatin, except for David
who takes the executioner's sword
and executes. Holding the hilt

in both hands, he severs
head from the rest of the stiff
and poses, weight on one foot,

contrapposto, his other foot on that boulder
of a head; one hand on the sword
and one on his hip, like a fashion shoot.

Why *not* flaunt it, with the invaders
in full rout. You know the rest:
the lord sends rain to settle the dust;

dogs wander through,
gnawing enemy corpses.

4. Caravaggio

As I recall, the boy has that
adolescent disdain. Lit by a candle
or the last of the sun, he holds
the severed head—its runny eyes

rolling up, lips like swollen worms
open over tombstone teeth.
Still bleeding out, it has not yet

gone gray, this grotesque of Caravaggio's
own head. Here, in the mirror that will not
compromise, is your pride.

Magdalene on the Bus

Wearing an odor of cut roses
rotting in a vase, she pushed up front
to seats reserved for the elderly,
sick, or pregnant. She was none,

or all the above. A remnant
of that famous hair flowed down her back.
Setting a mesh bag beside her—quarter kilo
bufala, a tenth of prosciutto—

she settled into the comfort
of a plastic seat. I used to see her
near Corso Vittorio Emanuele,
squatting with her coat, a few coins

scattered on it, spread before her
like a sleeping dog. She held
an arm to me, to help her stand.
Where you going, she said,

home? It was a small flat,
I was a guest. *Bene, bene,* she said.
This time I stood in the aisle,
hanging onto the strap,

doing a two-step with the others
each time the bus lurched
as she lifted her crusty feet
from her shoes. Slumming goddess,

or wayward saint with black
and missing teeth, she was the one
who grinned, the rest of us pretending
to stare straight ahead,

our fists clutching the bills
and coins in our pockets.

On Not Smiling

It is not that their teeth have gone bad,
or they hold down two jobs
that makes their gaze wander to the side in photos

as though bitten with a sudden tiredness,
nor an image of parents slogging back
from Germany after the war.

Even their grandmothers, as teenagers,
stood tight-lipped in those timed exposures.

Only sometimes, in private, a flicker
no camera will ever catch,
leaving no record they were ever lighthearted—

leaving the gods, on whatever Olympus remains,
without happiness as an excuse
when they decide to start punishing us again.

u kłada renka o opisania ton
szystko wymagało ciągno
y tam postać sam sobo roz mistl
misli i doradzi jak zostawić was
ach ale i na oczy mało zaciągnąć
m czasem pokornie dziękuje pa
cze przy dobrej pamięci żegnam
s wszystkich dla pana Jezusa
we utrzymały otkupienie co
nas wszystkich utrzymanie io
umrzem nie przyjęte modły i p
kościoły nie dawał żeby w domu
z rozmyślam w dzień i w nocy że
a ojczyzn Bog dobrotliwy wie c
ych kolegów nie ma o ktuen
zie Brastaskie pomierali s
tra kostoska rok temu jak um
e widziała taki nasz rodzaj z
as wszystkich Panu Bogu

November

> *non sono mai stato*
> *tanto*
> *attaccato alla vita*
> —Giuseppe Ungaretti, "Veglia"

> *This is a table I was saying*
> *this is a table*
> *on the table are lying bread a knife*
> —Tadeusz Różewicz, "In the Middle of Life"

I parked my car on the lawn.
The sky didn't stop being blue
or hard. I smoked a Camel.
Voices seeped like shadows
through the hum of power lines,

the future streaked with white-out.
My room, a mattress
on a layer of springs; a desk; words
on paper; a beehive of snow.

Even if I could start the car,
there was nowhere to go.
There is only one life,
I kept telling myself.

The basil had blackened
and disappeared into upright
threads. The rosemary held its own
against clear skies.

Morning became afternoon,
the sun, a hazelnut.
Azaleas put out buds for the future,

the new moon
held out empty arms. Nobody
had wiretapped the trees yet,
the leaves on the king crimson,
pretending to the throne,
lingered in the snake-bit air.

November. It snowed and melted,
old leaves layered the ground
like fermented squash. The sky,
falling on the far side of the river,

could only dream of being so yellow.
A little hornet flesh

remained in the heat of the Earl Gray.
Every day drifted the usual route downhill.
A few rose canes grappled
up the latticework

as though fleeing
(flooded mineshaft, burial
at sea, falling into destiny
to escape it).

Geese passed over in weary formations.
The dog, wandering in
to sniff my shit and urine,

couldn't deliver a diagnosis
or say when, if ever, I'd recover.

Having flushed the deaths I'd set in motion
down the confessional,

I could have been clouds
drifting like homeless blimps.
The moon, staying up, prowled
for a river or wine-dark sea
to take its weight.

Theseus,
bearing down on land, forgetting to swap out
the black sails, his father waiting
on the cliffs. . . .

The first tag-ends of snow
filled the twig-lined garden;
the mired clouds curled like a cat,
a lump in the bed.
I decided to live

on a day like this—the lot next to the house,
a path leading through
poison ivy, the skeleton of a squirrel
in a tree hollow
creeping back into
the nineteenth century. It must be

the black coffee of decaying leaves
keeps me awake. I neither sank
nor floated. In truth,
I don't know where I went.
Other than those rings, what can time
matter to a tree? Night,

with its taming insistence, held me
pressed against its heart.

In third grade I used a ballpoint
for math. Sister Leona, who taught
my father thirty years before, slapped my face, hard.

I had nerve, she said, to spoil her
(unspoken)
plan to start everyone with ink come January.

The decision to live
—later—
always retroactive.

I could be thankful
words didn't disappear
into the cloistered future

the white noise of terra incognita

like Pirithous, bound to the chair
of forgetting, nabbed trying to kidnap
Persephone.
Lord Hades, pretty quick

on his feet, plopped him down,
oh poop,
on said chair (along with Theseus,
later rescued by Heracles—only room

for one passenger on that back),
leaving Pirithous to gape alone

into the void hereafter.

The sheer pleasure
of outwitting monsters—I was never a match
for their strength—lives on

but after running
the Minotaur through in the endless
alley of his prison, his look

of uncomprehending
hurt—animal lust on top of a human body
I followed the yarn

out, how to say
fulfillment didn't last like
what led to it

one more struggle
behind me, her soft arms ahead
the girl I'd abandon to the gods

a night—no two—
of bliss followed by wailing
when she wakens to see

my black sail clutching wind
we won't hear under the creak
of our rigging, under the cloak

of forgetting

Dark came early to Spoleto, too,
in the chilled breath of the moon
where every house had not one cellar
but three going down
to the third century. The air stung
like the first Lucky Strike of the day.
I went to the bar,
drank cognac in one gulp as though
I could embrace the night. The joke is,
in some places you can dig and discover oil
like the Beverly Hillbillies.
Here, you get another ruin.

I could have stayed forever.
Maybe I did: in that
moment Giorgio fiddled
with his car, something about
the "motor tree,"
everyone pretending
Orlando ran the family.
We went outside to prove
we were alive. We drank
from artesian wells by the post office.
The moon sweated its light on us
and we shivered back.

When I decided to live,
they started a new war.
It was similar to the old one.

Waiting at a stop light
I watched a flock of pigeons
fold out of freezing rain
to the boulevard.

They thought there was nothing to lose—
easy in, easy out, and everyone
dancing in the streets—
the liberation of Paris all over again.

I wondered how pigeons
kept from icing up in the freezing rain.
I couldn't halt the invasion
or recall the troops,
or make them stop saying
Operation Iron Fist.

The rain kept falling.
What could fences matter to pigeons
flaunting the laws of aerodynamics?

No matter how many times I traveled
into the past,
the future, like passengers

abandoned on the tarmac, had to look after
itself. My heart, that relic, snored,
dragging the moon like a plow

across the window.
Heart in its nest of ventricles,
its wine-red sea.

When I decided to live,
the moon waxed.
A tango. A red sky.

There was snow.
The test for love
had yet to be invented.

Out of the gray sky
rain slaps my window.
The dog wakes to satisfy
an itch. The furnace fan kicks in
three seconds before ignition.
Out of the gray sky
rain falls by special appointment to the earth.
Some days I'm noisy
as a rusted-out muffler
coughing up the last
of a cold—a Chevy or Oldsmobile
having trouble starting.
One day I'll wear
a waterproof jacket
and waterproof shoes
and I'll come walking
on back to you.

The leaves, lawn-surfing,
called out the sun,

that timid. Gallardia and Shasta daisy
not dead so much as beyond it all.

Abandoned, the girl gazed from
where it is always too late.

A violin mourned. What use
were the honors pinned over my heart then,
or ever?

Women, whose robes the color of sunrise
and midnight billow like sails, walk

as far as the village fire station,
speaking with hands like Italians,

adjusting their head scarves
as though soothing the wind. Called to mourn

with their verses and bent backs,
with their knowledge of sins left unspoken,

they now drift
past burr oaks gone brown to cook rice

and goat from the corner market.
The shadows of branches on the wall,

in a wind made flesh, creep up
to congeal on the ceiling.

On the radio—25 dead Italians
in Iraq: car bomb. November sharpens

its claws across the frozen ground.
First sleet,
then a little sun. First wind,
then the wind of stars
and the hack-sawed moon.

I dug so many holes in the yard
this year—for trees, not grief—
but there's still room, if necessary,
to plant some grief.

What is the exact word for *sail*?
The word for *boulders*
beneath the cliff that breakers
pound?

What's the word for *pounding*
day and night, that gets in
my head, massaging my temples,
a whisper

in no known language?
The light has been strained
through cheesecloth,
the hundred things

to prepare for landing,
the returning youth—I among them—
intact or nearly so, carried out.
Out of these festivities

windows covered with black sheets,
women gathering to march
through the center of town,
across the fields;

their looks,
when I asked who it was for: *You*
have your nerve,
spat back.

The future wallowed
like a whale
eluding our nets.

If I tell you to stop,
will you keep going?

clicking like a cricket
after October
fades in forgotten leaves—

winter wheat, red clover,

we grow from seed.

I will carry my own wood from the shed,
a dog breaking the trail
through snow.
I will lift
myself into air, lower myself
to the ground.
I'll wear what fits best

I'll wear nothing at all.

ronisława a i uważam z nich t
n jak się obrócić niech Bronisła
szystkich bo co raz gorzej nie to co m
i spamiętnici codzień inaczej
Bogu i tobie zapamiętnić i apien
ię z wami i z całą rodziną polecz
tki Boskie i świętego Józefa

A Letter to Serafin

go świata to jest nay ważniejsze
na pokontrzyemy pożniej nie po
by i aby ło się za ceskąpstwo
to jak uważam dużo marnie poszło
eba stanąć przed sądem Bo-
m dłużej to twien kszepytanie.
rozmiawiał na Tonecwka by c
e i pani ozek jednego roky rodzi
ła ale sz nie znała nikogo
czerstwości nie ma polecam
ałą rodziną Zostaję życzliwy
Serafin minczesni

Wooden Pencils Are Born

Wooden pencils are born
with erasers. It is we
who chew them off.

That anything at all should happen
still amazes me: night wiping away
the landscape like a rag

on a blackboard, night
with its caravans; an ensuing dawn
(feeble, with clouds)

I've done nothing to earn.
The grass stays green
under the film of snow,

branches will leaf out
in four months, covering
all this sky.

Each morning I boil
water for coffee,
leaving the nail someone

will pound through my heart
behind the unopened curtain.

Once, in the boundary waters,
at the intersection of dinner
with luck, we cooked smallmouth fillets
in Alfredo sauce.

Time had invaded our store-bought
flatbread with a green powder
that carried it back to the beginning.

Travelers stranded, luggage lost,
the heater fan was the only thing running
between Christmas and New Year.

Leave me alone just now,
the dying woman, gathering herself,
said to her children.

The Last Pietà

Eighty years old, with little patience for fools
or himself, he smashed the virgin's arm
and the left leg of Jesus. Gone were the days
he could wrestle a David out of flawed marble;

the scaffolding he'd invented for the Sistine Chapel
had long been split for firewood. Maybe the marble
had gone bad, maybe the corpse showed too much
interest in the two Marys, but Nicodemus, straining

to lay the body in the Madonna's arms,
showed enough promise to wear Michelangelo's face and beard.
Pietà. The pity of it. The body of the god,

for the remaining eternity of stone, stays broken.
And the Virgin—her face gouged and unpolished, broad-cheeked
as a Polish peasant—she could be anyone's mother.

Maybe

I ask whether it's better to take the train
to Lublin, or a bus. "Maybe," she says,
"we'll take you in the car." Her father
has driven us for days: Białystok, Sokółka,

the farm my grandfather left at seventeen.
Maybe they will take us, after her classes,
in the little egg-sac of a blue car.
Maybe it will be her birthday present

and we will buy dinner for her
and her father. Maybe Joan will order
pork cutlets. They'll probably drive
back before dark over nicked

and gouged roads. There's a chance
it will start raining. Maybe
my sniffles are the onset of a cold.
In the tight nest of the car,

maybe she'll catch it. The last butterfly
of the season, sputtering across the road,
could splash against
the windshield. A horse drawn carriage

might clop along the slow lane of the highway.
Maybe it will be October. *Hello* and *goodbye,*
it happens, is the same word. On the hotel steps,
where we stand getting our picture taken,

I'm the American who's smiling
to show the future all is well.
Hello and goodbye. My cousins
are the ones whose eyes avoid the camera.

Lublin, Rain

Bank tellers sit behind their windows,
pushing paperwork
toward the end of day. In the museum,

workers polish swords of generals
who led one failed campaign
after another, my ancestors

trudging beside their horses.
And now, the wars having thinned,
umbrellas fill narrow streets.

On the castle's top floor, in a chapel
covered with frescos (visit of the magi,
Jesus, Mary, and all the saints),

a boy from the special school looks at me
with a drooping, flounder's eye.
Something in the histories of my face

makes him touch my arm
and run to the other gape-mouthed children,
no longer studying Byzantine art

of the fourteenth century, but me
—*it*—shadow
I'm dragging through your streets, Lublin.

Thieves of Warsaw

Stories surrounded you
like the miniscule heart of cyanide
in photographs:

how you flagged down tourists
as you stood by a dead Fiat
to hijack their rental;

how you sprayed sleeping-gas into train compartments
freeing us of earthly baggage,
easing our way into purgatory.

The paper cups of beggars are empty—
there is no espresso, no more Nescafé.
The leaves of cypresses have flown,

and you're waiting at the train station
for a taxi to arrive, a plump American
and his wife; thank Jesus

if they squabble like jackdaws
on escalators down to the platform.
Flipping your cigarettes to the curb,

you shadow them to the lowest level.
Overhead bulbs flicker before a train pulls in,
and only you, thieves, can see in the dark.

The Prisoners

Some tour guides use bullhorns to stand out.
Whether Michelangelo meant *to finish them*
is beside the point. It is American day at the Accademia;
we are all treated to English.

The Pope dragged him off to Rome
(by the ear, like a truant) *for the Sistine Fresco.*
He has captured the slaves (did I say *Prisoners*?)
red-handed, making a break from the rock.

Now they're stuck, abandoned by the man
who could have liberated them with mere taps
of a chisel. Blame the Pope. As long
as they have Christianity, these slaves,

what's the problem? One of them
still strains to pull the stone, like a too-tight sweater,
over his head. *Maybe we should be grateful*
the Pope yanked Michelangelo away at this point.

A kind of punishment, those four years
he spent stuck to the ceiling,
head cranked back, face spattered with paint.
One of the slaves has almost broken loose

from his imprisonment. Another seems,
behind his closed eyes, to be drifting back,
exhausted, into rock's long, sweet dream.

The Bones

did not swarm like gnats
at the end of summer,
or fling themselves against
my wallpaper like panicked bats.

Anchored under frost-heaved rock,
tree roots sniffed them out with the agility
of prospectors and alchemists
exploring delicate cracks,

translating grandfather oak,
grandmother maple into sap and leaves.
Reanimated in my nightly dream rushes,

he worked nights cleaning a light house;
she took me dancing, gave me checks
I could never cash. Mornings, they departed
under waves of amnesia and yearning.

They huddle together in the dark
at a near-constant 50 to 73 degrees Fahrenheit,
and I don't grind them into pigments
for artists needing *bone black* or *mummy brown,*

or distill them into a mother tincture
for anyone desperate enough for a cure,
anyone demanding eternity now.

Two White Bowls

After a painting by Jósef Czapski

Tomorrow they'll mate with yogurt,
sliced apples, the dash of cinnamon

she craves: coffee, the stain
of raspberries. Today,

adrift on the sea of the table,
without rudder, as Machado says,

they guard their emptiness
like stones rolled from the grave,

a portion of night
floating among the candelabra of stars.

What else would they give—

the still-singing head of Orpheus?
Or your own hands,

palms opened and waiting, the gift
about to arrive? Halves

of the moon—one fits
in your right hand, waxing,

the other slowly disappears in your left
on nights we crave darkness,

when *it is snowing and it is going to snow.*
What more did you expect? A clapper

to go inside the bells? On the far edge
of the table, the half-formed rim

of a bowl, like an incubating nebula:
for darkness comes first, then

a container for it. By now
it is turning dark, the green

of the forest has begun
to go blue. What more

did you expect—the sound
of villagers escaping?

Another ladleful
of watery nettle soup?

In a Spoleto Hotel

There's the sound of women
walking on pavement,
the sound of drills
and pigeons, always
pigeons, and a power saw
coming from the house
where someone puts a song together—
day after day, the same song,
playing back the tape,
noodling through new riffs
until it is perfect.
Will it ever achieve
greatness? There is only
this single, flexible moment:
pigeons on the roof
pecking at grass
between terra cotta tiles,
olive trees on the hill,
the same background
of a thousand paintings.
The sky is not the lapis
of God-the-father's robe
in the Fillippo Lippi fresco.
Not yet, but it will be
later tonight or
sometime tomorrow
after the clouds leave,
after we are gone.

A Letter to Serafin

Serafin, orphaned angel,
all that's left are a few pigs,
some rutabagas, and winter wheat.
Your great-grandchildren,

heirs to your legacy of dirt,
cultivate dialects like snow.
I am speaking from a suburb of St. Paul.
It is October. I am not raking

or composting. Nothing remains the same—
a galvanized roof shines on top of your house;
nobody has time for thatching anymore—
yet everything is the same.

The family, having gathered beets,
came from hunting mushrooms
to set out sausage and relishes.

What was I doing there, they asked,
how old was I? *More tea?*
Vodka? And everything made by hand—
you'd feel at home.

They laid out inventories from the war—
a hand blown off by a land mine in the field,
a father who walked home from Germany
more bone than flesh.

Bankruptcies keep filtering down—
stifled inheritances,
a grimace mistaken for a smile.

The animals remain—pigs, a cow staked out
in a field to graze—descended from those
you fed, who adored you,
whoever you were, Serafin.

Notes

"A Letter from My Great-Grandfather, Serafin Minczewski"

The references to Jelenie Góra indicate a hamlet of a half-dozen houses twenty or so kilometers from Białystock and not the large, much better known city of the same name.

I am indebted to Michał and Łucasz Łuczaj for translating the letter from Serafin Minczewski to my grandfather, ca. 1920.

"November"

The epigraph by Giuseppe Ungaretti translates literally as "…never have I been/so/attached to life." The epigraph by Różewicz is from a translation by Czesław Miłosz.

Pirithous was the Lapinth prince and Theseus' best friend. Theseus accompanied him to Hades to kidnap Persephone, but they were tricked by the god Hades into sitting on the chairs of forgetting and were held fast. One version of the story has it that Heracles, in Hades on one of his labors, saved Theseus by ripping him off the chair, leaving some flesh behind. This accounts for the legend that men of Athens have rather skinny asses.

"Two White Bowls"

The quote from Antonio Machado is from a poem that, roughly translated, goes:

> Four things are useless at sea:
> rudder, anchor, oars,
> and the fear of going down.

The quote by Wallace Stevens is from the final section of "Thirteen Ways of Looking at a Blackbird."

Art Referred to in Ekphrastic Poems

"Annunciation"

A composite based mainly on two *Annunciations* by Leonardo da Vinci, one in the Uffizi Gallery, Florence, and the other in the Louvre, Paris.

"Michelangelo: Leda and Zeus"
From the painting in the Galleria della Accademia, Florence.

"Relics"
The two reliquaries may be found in the Museo dell'Opera del Duomo, Florence.

"Prophet"
Donatello's sculpture of the prophet Habakkuk, originally in the Baptistry in Florence, is located in the Museo dell'Opera del Duomo. It is familiarly known as *lo Zuccone*, or "Pumpkin Head."

"Abraham"
Inspired by Caravaggio's *The Sacrifice of Isaac* in the Uffizi Gallery, Florence.

"Madonna with the Outline of a Breast"
Anonymous, 12th or 13th century, found in the Museo dell'Opera del Duomo.

"Judith and Holofernes"
Largely based on Artemisia Gentileschi's *Judith and Holofernes* in the Uffizi Gallery.

"The Davids"
Bernini—Galleria Borghese, Rome; Michelangelo—Galleria della Accademia, Florence; Donatello—Il Bargello Gallery, Florence; Caravaggio—Galleria Borghese, Rome.

"Magdalene on the Bus"
Loosely based on Donatello's wooden sculpture of Magdalene in the Museo dell'Opera del Duomo, Florence.

"The Last Pietà," "The Prisoners"
Michelangelo's sculptural groupings, *Pietà* and *The Prisoners* are both in the Galleria della Accademia, Florence.

Acknowledgments

I'd like to thank the editors of the following journals and presses for publishing earlier versions of poems that appear in this book:
Cerise Press: "On Not Smiling"
Connecticut Poetry Review: "Farm, 1962," "Michelangelo: Leda and Zeus," "October Primrose"
Crab Orchard Review: "Thieves of Warsaw"
Fourth River: "A Letter to Serafin," originally published as "A Letter to Serafin M."
Great River Review: "Jewish Cemetery, Rymanów"
The Isle Review (defunct online journal): "Lublin, Rain"
Marlboro Review: "Resort Town"
Meridian: "Tree Lilac in Blossom," originally published as "Japanese Tree Lilac on Solstice (4)"
Mid-American Review: "Two White Bowls"
Mr. Cogito (online at www.mrcogito.freeservers.com): "November," from "The Camps" sequence
Poetry East: "Out of the gray sky..." originally titled "on listening to Robert Johnson's Blues"
Poetry Midwest: "On the radio—25 dead Italians..."
Quarterly West: "A Letter from My Great-Grandfather, Serafin Minczewski"
Sojourn: "One Version," "In a Spoleto Hotel"
Umbrella: "The Last Pietà," "Madonna with the Outline of a Breast"
"Annunciation" originally appeared in a postcard series published by Červená Barva Press.
"A Letter to Serafin" was included in a special issue of *Kritya,* focusing on Polish-American Poets.
The fourth section of this book, "November," was published as a limited edition chapbook by Finishing Line Press, Lexington, Ky., 2007.

Travel and time to write were made possible by generous grants from the Saint Paul Companies and the Jerome Foundation. Many thanks also to the Corporation of Yaddo and the Anderson Center for Interdisciplinary Studies for the use of their facilities where I worked on a number of these poems.

Additional thanks to those who have read and commented on earlier versions of these poems and manuscript: Kath Jesme, Alvaro Cardona-Hine, Eleanor Wilner, Carlen Arnett, Ed Shannon, Becca Barniskis, Patricia Zontelli, Janet Holmes, Bob Ayres, Francine Sterle, Elton Glaser, John Guzlowski, Philip Metres, my editor, Mary Biddinger, and the anonymous reviewers at the University of Akron Press.

I'd like to thank Józef, Grazyna, and Joanna Kuryłowicz for their generosity, help, and hospitality in Czarna Białystocka, Poland, and my cousin Jadwiga Ejsmont for arranging introductions; Sarah, Łukasz, and Michał Łuczaj in Krosno, Poland; Monika Garbowska in Lublin. To Topazia Alliata and Toni Mariani in Rome, undying gratitude.

Akron Series in Poetry

Mary Biddinger, Editor

Barry Seiler, *The Waters of Forgetting*
Raeburn Miller, *The Comma After Love: Selected Poems of Raeburn Miller*
William Greenway, *How the Dead Bury the Dead*
Jon Davis, *Scrimmage of Appetite*
Anita Feng, *Internal Strategies*
Susan Yuzna, *Her Slender Dress*
Raeburn Miller, *The Collected Poems of Raeburn Miller*
Clare Rossini, *Winter Morning with Crow*
Barry Seiler, *Black Leaf*
William Greenway, *Simmer Dim*
Jeanne E. Clark, *Ohio Blue Tips*
Beckian Fritz Goldberg, *Never Be the Horse*
Marlys West, *Notes for a Late-Blooming Martyr*
Dennis Hinrichsen, *Detail from* The Garden of Earthly Delights
Susan Yuzna, *Pale Bird, Spouting Fire*
John Minczeski, *Circle Routes*
Barry Seiler, *Frozen Falls*
Elton Glaser and William Greenway, eds., *I Have My Own Song for It: Modern Poems of Ohio*
Melody Lacina, *Private Hunger*
George Bilgere, *The Good Kiss*
William Greenway, *Ascending Order*
Roger Mitchell, *Delicate Bait*
Lynn Powell, *The Zones of Paradise*
Dennis Hinrichsen, *Cage of Water*
Sharmila Voorakkara, *Fire Wheel*
Kurt Brown, Meg Kearney, Donna Reis, Estha Weiner, eds., *Blues for Bill: A Tribute to William Matthews*
Vern Rutsala, *How We Spent Our Time*
Clare Rossini, *Lingo*
Beckian Fritz Goldberg, *The Book of Accident*

Ashley Capps, *Mistaking the Sea for Green Fields*
Roger Mitchell, *Half / Mask*
Alison Pelegrin, *Big Muddy River of Stars*
Jeff Gundy, *Spoken among the Trees*
Brian Brodeur, *Other Latitudes*
William Greenway, *Everywhere at Once*
Heather Derr-Smith, *The Bride Minaret*
John Gallaher, *Map of the Folded World*
John Minczeski, *A Letter to Serafin*

About the Author

John Minczeski resides in the Twin Cities, where he works and teaches. The author of four poetry collections and the editor of three anthologies, his poems have appeared in numerous journals, including *Poetry East, Quarterly West, Agni, Meridian, Pleiades, Free Lunch,* and *Nowa Okolica Poetow.* His book, *Circle Routes,* won the Akron Poetry Prize in 2000.

About the Book

A Letter to Serafin was designed and typeset by Amy Freels. The typeface, Centaur, was designed by Bruce Rogers. It was released in 1929 by the Monotype Corporation.

A Letter to Serafin was printed on 60-pound Glatfelter Offset Natural and bound by Cushing-Malloy of Ann Arbor, Michigan.